CONFESSIONS
OF A FOOL

DILLINGHAM'S AMERICAN AUTHORS LIBRARY, No. 11.

FEBRUARY, 1896. ISSUED MONTHLY. $6 PER YEAR.
ENTERED AT THE NEW YORK POST OFFICE AS SECOND-CLASS MATTER.

CONFESSIONS

OF A FOOL

As Made by Himself.

NEW YORK:

COPYRIGHT, 1895, BY

G. W. Dillingham, Publisher,

MDCCCXCV.

ISBN: 978-1-6673-0523-3 paperback
ISBN: 978-1-6673-0524-0 hardcover

CONTENTS

CHAPTER I.

STOPPING A GAP

The fact that the Widow was going to be there was enough for me although 1 well understood that I was asked on the trip for something else than to be with the Widow. I do not fool myself on this point. Faxon would take care of the Widow. I was to take care of the Widow's sister. Well, Faxon owns the yacht and may arrange these little things as he pleases. He wants to own the Widow, and some one must be on hand to absorb the sister for the Widow never goes far afield without her sister.

The sister attachment lends respectability and dullness to our sojourn.

Still, if I didn't fill the gap, Faxon would simply invite some other fellow. After all, if I don't get the Widow, there are patés – and Faxon's steward does make a sublime paté and no end of champagne. Besides, I have a suspicion that the Widow would prefer my company to Faxon's. That is something only the yacht is Faxon's, and the Widow must needs go with it.

It's hard work, though, not to violate the confidence of my host. How will I recall the sail two weeks ago!

When the Widow came back down the companion-way after dinner that evening, ostensibly to get her wrap, and finding me waiting at the foot of the ladder for her asked me to fetch the wrap from her state-room, and then let me lay it over her shoulders, and, somehow, allowed her face to come so near mine that I got the fragrance from the poudre on her cheekwell, nothing but the most absurd strength of purpose prevented me from holding on to her for the rest of the run home and letting Faxon indulge himself with the sister and the sulks. As it was, I'm afraid I went so far that there would have been no more yachting trips for me if the Widow had not subsequently got the sister to particularly request my company on board!

* * * *

I know, as a matter of fact, that I made a mess of it yesterday. The Widow was particularly fascinating. She has reduced her mourning from the broad and somber

Stopping a Gap

border that distinguished her yachting suit earlier in the season, to a narrow edging of black about collar, cuffs and the hem of her skirt; and while thus modified, the outfit is not so conspicuously fetching, it pleasantly suggests a transition to a more properly approachable stage.

We had had usual weather since leaving the anchorage in the morning until after sundown in the evening. Then the breeze freshened remarkably and we took in topsails, and, by nine o'clock, had a reef in the mainsail. Faxon and I were helping the men at the running gear, and Faxon slipped and turned his ankle. Think he took too many cocktails before dinner his steward mixes a terrific cocktail. At the solicitation of the Widow he went below and turned in on top of one of the saloon transoms. I have reason to believe that he wanted the Widow to come down and nurse him, but she shuddered and said she could never bear to witness suffering and painbut that her sister was a splendid nurse. So the sister rubbed Faxon's ankle with liniment all the way home.

The Widow and I sat under the weather rail in the gloom and got along nicely. I wrapped her about with Faxon's big uniform overcoat, and, as she insisted I must be cold, I shared the overcoat with her.

It was all very pleasant until Faxon went off to sleep and the Widow's sister came on deck.

I'm afraid that when the club cruise starts I shall not be a guest on Faxon's yacht; but I wouldn't have missed that evening's experience for a dozen cruises. Besides, the Widow assures me by note this morning that unless there is another gentleman in the party she shall decline to go on the cruise.

That means me–I'm sure of it.

She has a nice way of putting things without really committing herself.

CHAPTER II.

A CHANCE ACQUAINTANCE

It's odd how a fellow with, brains in his head will so often consider it desirable amusement to get drunk.

Practical experience, covering a somewhat lengthy period, coupled with a conscientious consideration devoted to the subject during many despondent hours, leads me to the conclusion that the first drink is responsible for it all. While the first drink is rarely taken with a view to getting drunk, it too often leads directly, and by rapid stages, to that regrettable end.

Accordingly, I argue that avoidance of the first drink makes temperance an easy virtue to practice.

In other words, for me at least, it is as easy to be a Prohibitionist as to be a temperance man.

CONFESSIONS OF A FOOL

A cocktail before breakfast, before lunch, before dinner, or a social glass between meals the result is all the same with me. Other drinks are pretty sure to follow with an ever-decreasing interval between. I used to refrain from taking anything before evening, but had to abandon this apparently salutary practice – since it usually compelled me to sit up all night before getting in enough to go to bed on. Then I would rise with difficulty on the morning following, and, of necessity, take frequent bracers all day to do business on. The practice robbed me of sleep and unfitted me for work as well. Now I drink as early in the day as may be desired by any of my many friends – not even waiting for the hour when the sun gets over the foreyard, as is the rule, I believe, rigidly adhered to among naval men, who have an international fame for scientific intemperance. The result is, I retire early on my *otium cum dig.*, and enjoy a good night's rest, awakening on the morrow refreshed and ready for my day's toil.

Some days, to be sure, this practice raises the deuce with my day's toil, but there is no remedy except strict prohibition and that is only to be considered during hours of extreme remorse.

I am moved to write these philosophic lines because I sat up quite late last evening, and as nearly as I can recall myself, as I was, I drank too much.

A Chance Acquaintance

If I hadn't drunk too muck I would not have dropped into the dance hall where I found myself shortly before midnight.

And if I hadn't dropped into the dance hall I should not have met let me see, I believe she told me her name was Helen.

The dance was all right, and Helen, or any other young woman, had a perfect right to be there. It was the festival of some society, or military company, or something of that sort. The young women were there to dance and have a good time in a perfectly respectable, if not altogether high-toned, way. The young men, however, were there chiefly to empty a punch-bowl two or three times over and smoke cigarettes. Of course they danced,, but the intermissions were longer than the dances, because the young men, and not the young women, were running the affair. Then there were a lot of fellows and men about town who dropped in late in the evening, and most of them had done a goodly amount of drinking outside the hall – as I had.

I was impressed with Helen. She was exceedingly pretty, although when I try to picture her I can only see a pair of very large and very soft eyes. I cannot recall their color. I like to think of her as having an artistic temperament – judging from my recollection of her eyes.

Just about as I had come to regard her with interest she disappeared in the cloakroom. When she came out she had on her outer garments, apparently prepared to leave the dance.

A young fellow met her at the door of the cloak room. He was the kind of a young fellow whose ideas of being a man are gained by standing up against a bar. He bad had as much of the punch as he could reasonably carry, and was evidently a little proud of it. Indeed, he was disposed to show himself a reckless man of the world in the presence of Helen.

"You told me, Jack," I heard Helen say, "that you would take me home at midnight."

"Oh, pshaw!" remonstrated the young fellow; "the fun's just begun and Minnie doesn't want to go yet."

"I can't help it," pleaded Helen. "You know mother would be awful angry if I should stay until the ball ended. I'm going home, and if you won't go with me I shall go alone. You and Minnie may stay." The young fellow muttered something that sounded disagreeable, and then he turned on his heel and sauntered across the floor.

The girl stood irresolute a moment. Then she made her way to the main exit and passed out of the hall.

A Chance Acquaintance

I couldn't help following her. I liked to fancy myself as a sort of unknown protector of Helen's footsteps for the immediate future.

The sidewalk in the immediate vicinity of the doorway was ornamented with a group of young chaps who were refreshing their brows in the cool air and puffing cigarettes. When Helen had run the gantlet of their searching eyes she became the subject of a discussion which resulted in one of the group leaving his fellows and walking leisurely after her.

I sauntered after the young fellow.

Helen increased her steps, the young fellow increased his, and I kept the pace.

Finally the young fellow overtook Helen and accosted her. I slowed down to watch developments, and was rather pleased to observe that Helen did not take kindly to the company of the young fellow. After a little she stopped short and I heard her express herself to the effect that she would stand there for the rest of the night if the young fellow didn't go about his business. The recollection of this impresses me that Helen has a will as well as being artistic. The young fellow was expostulating when I overtook them, and I grabbed him by the collar and gave him a gentle twist and a shove that landed him in the gutter.

CONFESSIONS OF A FOOL

The girl looked up in my face an instant as if in doubt how to accept my appearance on the scene.

"I will go with you as far as may be necessary to save you from annoyance," I remarked, at the same time regretting that the situation had not found me perfectly free from the effects of the drinking that had occupied me during the earlier evening hours.

Helen looked straight up into my face with the expression of a girl who was perfectly able to take care of herself, but at the same time would be glad to be relieved of the responsibility if she could accomplish it judiciously. The inspection seemed to satisfy her. She was certainly not over twenty-one or twenty-two, and I am thirty-three; and very likely the discrepancy in our years gave her confidence, for she turned and walked along with me, without, however, accepting my proffered arm.

I don't recall much that we talked about on the way, although once she had placed her confidence in me so far as to let me walk with her, she began to chat freely and about all sorts of things that are interesting to a girl of her years dances and fellows and immature ideas of life, and the circus, and the work at which she was employed, and gossip about people that I never knew or expect to know. She explained that the "Jack" who had declined to take her home was her brother, and that he was keeping company with another young woman, for whose sake he wanted to remain at the ball.

I do remember that when I left Helen on the steps of a little cottage a long way from the scene of the ball, she extended her hand and, looking me frankly in the face with her big eyes, thanked me for being so kind to her.

She was not an uncommon sort of a girl, perhaps, but somehow I wished I might hold her hand for a week.

CHAPTER III.

KATE

"Are you sure you don't neglect your business through being too much of a good fellow, Dick?"

My sister put that interesting question to me the other evening. My sister is Mrs. Edward Marberry. She is a charming woman, although I never admired her taste in marrying Edward Marberry. I don't know how better I may describe Marberry than to remark that, in all his life, nobody ever referred to him as "Ned" Marberry. I know no other man of my acquaintance by the Christian name of Edward whom somebody – some one body, at least doesn't call "Ned." I never could contemplate with pleasure so anomalous a thing, any more than I could the character of a man named Charles, who would never be called "Charlie"; or what kind of a fellow it would be who would not be known as "Tom" if his name was Thomas.

19

Kate

Edward Marberry goes to bed every night at ten o'clock, and rises every morning at seven o'clock. He is down street to business by 8:30, and hasn't eaten a dinner or supper out of his house since he was married excepting on occasions when his college society holds its annual reunion, when, to my perennial surprise, he is always chosen to preside, and is esteemed the brightest fellow in the company. I understand he delivered the address to undergraduates on his class day at the university, and from old associates have heard it said that in his youth he was a tearing good fellow. I can't conceive of it, however. He has backslid terribly.

And yet I must acknowledge that. Marberry always dresses like a gentleman, and I'll wager the clothes on his back are paid for – with the cash discount. He certainly has provided a charming home for my sister, who, despite the fact that, as I remember her when she was a "young lady" and I a small boy, she was a particularly lively girl, fond of society and all that, she seems to be not only content, but actually happy in her humdrum married existence. I believe he takes her to everything that is first-class at the theatres, and she drives a good horse in an unostentatious sort of hitch-up, and gives afternoon teas, which her husband attends. I can't explain in detail why I think Marberry and she should not be happy; but if theirs is the right kind of a way to secure happiness in life, then my methods ought not to secure it, for they are diametrically opposite to Marberry's.

And yet, I'll bet no man on earth leads a Jollier life than I do.

But Kate – my sister – takes me to task occasionally – which means every time I run in to eat or loaf. She thinks I am wasting my career, whatever that may be. I tell her the only thing I waste is money, and there is plenty of -that in the world, if you can find a way to get hold of it honestly – and I have usually secured my share without too much work.

"You know, Dick," she said on this particular evening, "I have promised you never to refer again to your greatest error – to never recall to you your cruelty. The one thing you have done, which, as a woman, is a horror to me, I have ceased to speak to you about, but you must let me appeal to your good sense to take care of yourself, however careless you may be of others. You are my brother, Dick; I would have you manly and upright, and I hope you are, as the world outside looks at you. But, whether you are so regarded or not, I want you to take care of yourself."

"In other words, Kate," I interrupted, grimly, "you don't want me to make a fool of myself."

Kate

"I don't mean that exactly," returned this sweet woman. "I don't suppose you will ever do that or at least nobody will know it, because you are bright and smart. But what I am afraid of is, you will wreck yourself. You are too easy. You know you are, dear. It seems to me as if you would never stop being a boy. Everybody speaks of you as a 'good fellow/ but I am not sure that the good fellows are the kind that make successes of themselves. And, moreover, I don't know as it is always a long step from being what men call a good fellow to being what heart and conscience would recognize as a very bad fellow."

"Oh, Kate!" I expostulated. "I wouldn't talk like that. I never harmed anybody but myself."

"We won't discuss that," returned my sister, calmly, "because you know we differ on that point. I feel that you have harmed one other person, and harmed her grievously. Now, don't get up to go ; I don't mean to pursue that subject. Only this, you cannot well harm yourself without harming some one else, a little bit at least. Nobody is independent of others in this world. And if you could, you have no business to harm yourself. It is your business to take care of yourself. To secure a good name and an honorable position especially when God has given you talents enough to do it."

"I suppose you think I'll fill a drunkard's grave, or kill somebody, or rob a bank," I uttered, with an attempt at flippancy.

"Oh, Dick, you musn't laugh at me when I talk to you. Take me a little bit seriously for your own sake. You are too goodhearted to be vicious, too bright to intentionally destroy your reputation or yourself, and, of course, you are honest. I don't propose to insult you. But you are careless and reckless, and you don't care enough for yourself. You like a good time and good company, and you like them all the time. Now, there are some serious things in life to be attended to, and some serious hours to be passed and some serious duties to be performed, never mind how easy your pathway of life may seem to be. You may, perhaps, get through life without violating the liking of men and of women, and yet without securing a bit of their respect and esteem. And if you haven't that, you may depend upon it, brother, you will suffer your own self some time – suffer keenly, however happy a front you may present to the world."

"Well, well, Kate," I cried, "what a splendid preacher you would make!"

"Maybe so," said Kate, thoughtfully. "I don't think much else is necessary for preaching if you have sincerity. That is about all there is worth having, it seems to me. You may fool others, but you cannot fool yourself, Dick. That is the way Edward puts it – it is not original with me. And I hope you are not trying to fool yourself, brother."

My dear Kate! I rise from the great easy chair and cross the bit of space between us to her side. I take both her hands in mine, and she, too, rises, and I kiss her.

How sweet she is, with her soft, dark hair evenly parted and brought down on either side of her forehead, like a Madonna. I think it is of a Madonna she reminds me; my art education is very limited. I am proud of my sister, though, and I love her.

CHAPTER IV.

THE BOY
AND THE MAN

Well, I've seen Helen again.

She evidently regards me in the light of a hero.

I used to regard myself that way. But it has been many years since I or any one else has. It's rather pleasant to talk and walk with Helen under the circumstances. To be sure, she does most of the talking. A young girl is about the biggest chatterer on earth.

To talk with Helen carries me back to the younger days – the days when a fellow is really more of a man than he ever is in his life, I think, although he doesn't know it, but yearns for the time to come when he will have acquired more smoothness of physique and can lay claim to experiences. He would cover the fresh color in his cheeks with a beard, and would even like to have a gray hair or two in the beard. Proud as he is of his health and his strength, he would prefer the suggestion of a paunch to his flat stomach, and envies not a little the slight stoop of the shoulders which lends to that gray-mustached man he sees on the street a something that indicates the man-of-the-world, the chap who has suffered as well as enjoyed.

All this the boy would be to the girl he is fond of. He does not want to have her regard him too much as a boy. And he fools himself with the idea that he is a man of the world after all, and that she thinks so. Hasten the years! Hurry up the experiences! I want to be older!

Poor fool of a boy! Don't you remember the occasions when you dropped your absurd mask? Don't you remember the walk down the country road, when you turned a handspring over the five-barred gate, just to show off to her what a lithe young fellow you were? Don't you remember teaching her to swim, and how she remarked on the big muscles of your arms which swelled as you lifted her on your shoulder?

And you remember and smile, because of the pain it gave you, that night when you undertook to tell her that you loved her, and the fine words assembled from a dozen summer novels went out of your head before her swimming eyes looking up into yours. And at the supreme moment, when you were to have been so manly in your devotion, you were a blundering boy!

You are, indeed, older now. The fine words you couldn't say that night you could easily speak now exactly as the summer novelist writes them. You have had one or two experiences since then, and if you had that love scene to do over again, you would do it with neatness and despatch; and, after it was over, you would not have to feel afraid lest she thought you nothing but a boy for making such a mess of it, or kicking yourself because, in the moment's mad joy, when she had fallen into your arms, you had shut your eyes and kissed the back of her neck, instead of her waiting lips.

You recall that distinguished-looking man with the cameo-like face, smooth shaven always, the calm, steel-gray eyes, the silken hair, with a few streaks of gray in it, always immaculately dressed, strolling on the hotel piazza, while you were knocking about in a flannel shirt. Somehow that man had a peculiar attractiveness for her and for most of the young women about the hotel. The truth to tell, he was your ideal, too. Some day you would see the world and grow to be like him. But now, in self-defense, you scorned him. What could the girls see in that "old man" that they must all flock about him at every opportunity? A lithe young fellow like you could knock him down with a straight lefthander easily. Thank Heaven, you were young and had health and strength! Nevertheless you got out of your neglige for dinner so long as he stayed at the hotel.

Youth is no more sincere than age. Indeed, youth knows not the value of sincerity. Age does, even if it does not practice it. And some day you may grow old enough to realize, as Kate urges upon me, that there is not much else worth cherishing beside sincerity. The earlier you have learned that, the better for you.

And now I am nearly of the age that, when I was eighteen, I looked forward-to. I am of the age when it is easy to talk with a woman over twenty-five and embarrassingly delightful and reminiscence-producing to be alone with a schoolgirl. I can exchange flatteries and fall in love without much difficulty. And I know that the best and truest love a man ever feels is when he is a "boy" and is fond of a "girl." It may be love without reason and may not stand the test of marriage, but the boy is never to know again anything half so delectable. And it is a delight for the man to be taken back to the boy-days, as the walk and the talk with Helen take me back.

You have set me to thinking of all this, Helen. You, with your sweet chatter, talking to me as if you thought it your duty to entertain me, and, being unsophisticated (though you think you are not), you have an idea that what interests you must interest me and every one else. Your eyes are bright, your voice is pleasant to hear, and it is a delight to listen to you and to look at you. I wish I were a boy again. I haven't the heart to pay you compliments, and I don't know what else to talk about to you. It isn't very necessary for me to say anything at all, for you have a big fund of things to talk about, just as another sweet little woman and I used to have in common, until we began to make love to one another. And then we had that to talk about, and that was enough. She was a high-bred woman, and you, Helen, are a girl that works for your living. Perhaps you are high-bred, too. You certainly are fairly educated, Helen, as rich and poor may be in our land, and you are bright and smart. I like you. I think Kate, my sister, might like you. And the Widow would be jealous of you.

I would as life the Widow would know I like to talk and walk with you, Helen.

I am not so sure that I should like to tell Kate about you.

CHAPTER V.

A PARADOXICAL DIVERSION

It's odd how a fellow will be proud of the fact that he has lost a pile of money gamely. Any one may boast of his winnings, but real sporting blood is evidenced only by the complacency – even satisfaction – with which you are able to face your losings.

For example, I pretended to the same hilarity when I dropped my last available dollar on the last event at the track to-day as I used to feel when, as a youngster at college, I thought it smart to "go broke" at a silly roulette wheel or to stake my last cent on a bluff at poker that I was sure was going to be called.

It has been a great week. Wonderful, the excitement of exchanging a roll of greenbacks for a vari-colored ticket; then promenading the paddock puffing a strong

cigar, with the indescribable self -consciousness of playing a goodly stake outwardly calm, inwardly – confess
it – 'burning up for forty-five minutes waiting for the
event to be started! Zip! In forty-five seconds the short
furlongs are covered, and you are at liberty to joke with
your friends about the evaporation of another fifty. The
degree of complacency marks the drops of real sporting
blood in your veins. It is so nice to be known as a real
sport, and the only test is to lose.

Your nightcap – of coure it is whiskey, the only liq-
uor on earth for a nightcap until you enter upon the bran-
dy periodsets your brain a-going, when you would have
thought you had drunk enough during the evening to put
you into a sow's slumber. And you may lie on your bed,
your eyes staring wide open into the darkness, and think
of how much drudgery it took to enable you to indulge in
the delight of throwing away that fat roll of greenbacks!
Thank God, you are not such a damn fool as Faxon, who
lit his cigar with a crisp certificate just before the party
broke up. You didn't have a bill left to burn.

And your debts, too that roll of bills might have tak-
en some of them off your conscience for you have a conscience and are ashamed yet to face the man to whom
you owe money.

A pistol might be handy at this time!

A Paradoxical Diversion

But no – don't take yourself too seriously. You are a fool, that's all, and so long as most people don't know it, you can afford to laugh at yourself.

Only, remember, some day people will begin to find it out! And when they do, you will discover that yon are likely to be regarded a knave as well. You'll have to stop, old man, if you don't want to face that.

Now your eyelids will close at last. The lightning-like effect of the nightcap is working off. Your brain is quieting down. You will hold a calmer, if no better, opinion of yourself in the morning. There's plenty of chance yet to straighten yourself out before your friends discover what a sham you are.

"I observe," remarked the Widow, as I joined her in the grand stand, "that you have a new and very pretty acquaintance."

"To whom do you refer?"

"Dear me! how sly of you! I don't know her name but – she is young and pretty, and as I have seen you on two successive days on the street with her I'm afraid that I shall have less of your company in the future."

"You got along well enough without my company on the cruise," I remarked, viciously.

"Oh, no, dear, I did not. You see, I am frank with you. I admit that, pleasant as the cruise was, I should have enjoyed it far better with you on board. You know I like your company, or I wouldn't have accepted so much of it. It isn't pleasant to be dropped by one's old friends a woman likes flattery too well for that, you know." "I don't know whether you are laughing at me or not."

"Then your perceptions are lacking in their accustomed brilliancy. Of course, I am laughing at you. You don't imagine for a moment that I am going to cry over you? Go ahead, make some little creature like that black-haired young girl fall in love with you. It will be easy enough, I'm sure. Any man can make almost any woman think she's in love with him if he goes about it right – providing, always, that he is fairly prepossessing and has decent manners. A male flirt is an abomination, of course, but it takes my sex a long while to recognize the flirts if they are only kind to them."

"You are inclined to be mischievous, today," I venture to remark. "Can't a fellow be seen on the street with a woman without being accused of trying to flirt with her? or, worse yet, of trying to make love to her?"

"You can't – not two days in succession," remarked the Widow, with a disagreeable laugh.

I shut up. The horses are off. Our glasses are on them. It's a steeplechase, and, if I had any money upon it, it would be exciting. Fortunately, one of the riders is

A Paradoxical Diversion

thrown, and a little interest is accordingly aroused. I forget a good many other things as I watch the trackmen pick the little jockey up. There is a prolonged cheer. Somebody's horse has won. I have no money on the event and so watch the inanimate little body, in the yellow shirt being borne across the track to the stables. A small part of the crowd of thousands move over in that direction. A whisper runs through the crowd that a jockey has been badly hurt – killed, perhaps.

"How exasperating!" says a harsh voice in my ear. It is the Widow speaking.

"What's the matter now?"

"I had a ticket on that horse. He was sure to win, but of course that stupid jockey couldn't stay on his back!"

CHAPTER VI.

MOLLIE HAYDEN

"Dear Richard," my sister wrote – she usally writes "Richard," instead of "Dick." Indeed, except when talking to me earnestly about myself, and affectionately, she invariably addresses me as "Richard." It's a delicate way she has of indicating her respect for me, coupled, I always feel, with the suggestion that I respect myself that I grow up to "Richard."

"Dear Richard – Come over to dinner with us Wednesday evening. Miss Hayden, a cousin of Mr. Marberry's, and her mother are to be our guests for a week on their return home from the Pier. You will have to help me entertain them. I know I may depend upon you."

Depend upon me! Well, I should say so! Pm accustomed to being "depended upon." Didn't do a stroke of work all summer because so many persons depended upon me! And the winter has started in before the autumn is half gone, with more engagements than even I feel prepared to tackle. The club, the lodge, the dancing crowd – I don't dare contemplate how many committees Pm on to do this and to do that and to get up this and to get up that and all fun and a good time. The devil only knows where Pm coming out. I didn't earn enough money last Spring to even carry me through the summer, and I've got to buckle down to work sooner or later or Dun's man will be crowding me again as he did three years ago, when I went to Europe for a month and spent a year's time and no end of money on that yellowheaded singer in Berlin.

But Kate, you shall not be neglected while I have an hour or a penny to spare. That husband of yours is about as much help for an entertainer as a cigar-store Indian. Your brother is worth something in this world, after all, isn't he, Kate? Once in a while, as a convenience to be "depended upon!"

* * * *

Well, I've had a surprise party!

Mollie Hayden is a resplendent beauty. I suspected that, because Kate didn't say a word about her in her letter. Ned Marberry has broken me up completely, too. We enjoyed a very pleasant evening Wednesday. I was greatly impressed with Marberry's cousin. She had met a lot of people at the Pier that I had known in past seasons, and she didn't give any sign that they had told her too much about me – or, indeed, had even mentioned me for the matter of that. She is a thorough young woman of the world. Not like the Widow. The Widow is tough. But just a wellpoised, handsome, wholesome girl, who may have a love affair to her account, perhaps, and knows how to be perfectly free without being frivolous or silly.

Let me look back over the week. It's been mighty jolly – only that confounded Marberry violated all my confidence in him as a dyed-in-the-wool chump. Shouldn't wonder if he might be a good fellow if he wanted to be. During the evening, Wednesday, I invited everybody to take in the theatre with me Thursday night, and then we had a little supper, and I'm blessed if Marberry didn't indulge himself in the champagne. On Friday, Marberry took us all out for an old-fashioned roughing – a trip up-country in his trap – I didn't know he owned a trap before. Mollie Hayden and I sat together on the back seat and I had a distinctly jolly time. On Saturday Kate gave a complimentary tea to her guests, which would have been extraordinarily dull if Marberry hadn't rigged up a little spread in the smoking room for us fellows after the affair was over. Said he didn't get any satisfaction from sweet crackers and bonbons himself, and knew we fellows must be hungry. He actually produced a couple of bottles of Burgundy that he admitted had been lying in his cellar ever since he was married. That shows his slowness. I wouldn't wonder but Marberry was quite a boy after all in his younger days before he backslid.

Sunday we all went to church twice, morning and evening service. Don't remember when I have been to church before. But I would go anywhere with a girl like Mollie Hayden.

Monday afternoon I hired a Victoria and took the folks about town and out to the Park. Marberry couldn't go – business. Was glad of it for that matter. Would just as lief as not be the only fellow in a party that included Mollie Hayden.

In the evening we had dinner *en famille,* with a little music. Miss Hayden plays a viola exquisitely, and she sings, too has a pure contralto voice. I know I would give a good deal to have her voice around the house all the time. I remarked as much to Kate the other day and she reminded me gently that as sweet a voice as Mollie Hayden's had once been mine to listen to.

Tuesday night we saw a bit of light opera and after returning home Kate made a rarebit and Marberry actually had some Bass to go with it. I believe Marberry would make quite a decent sort of a chap if he would let himself loose.

The Haydens departed Wednesday forenoon. I saw them off on the train Kate and I. We had driven down in the democrat, and I drove back home with Kate, stopping on the way for her to do some shopping. Kate didn't speak to me during the ride. When we reached the house she invited me to come in and I went in. I followed her into the drawing room. She stepped in front of the mirror, unconsciously regarding her handsome face as she deliberately drew off her gloves from as snug a pair of hands as there is in the world.

She turned to me after a moment.

"Dick," she said, looking me straight in the eye, "I didn't tell the Hay dens much about you."

"Thank you," I returned, inclined to feel amused, but estopped from expressing the inclination by my sister's perfectly serious face.

"They are very nice people," pursued my sister, her eyes dropping a moment as she neatly folded her gloves and laid them on the mantel under the mirror.

"Miss Hayden is certainly charming," I ventured to remark.

"Decidedly so," said my sister. "They are very well to do, the family connections are very nice, and ''

My sister paused and, facing the mirror, began to draw the pins out of her hat.

"Kate," I said, after watching her a moment, "I may have to go West on a business trip shortly. Wouldn't it be perfectly proper to renew my acquaintance with the Haydens by stopping over a few days?"

"They would he very glad to see you, I am sure," said my sister. "They both feel, as I do, under great obligations to you for paying them so much attention during their stay with us, and I am confident they would be glad to reciprocate your kindness."

Kate had by this time got her hat unpinned, and I stepped to her to assist in removing her light jacket.

"Will you stop to luncheon, Richard?" she asked, as she turned herself out of the jacket and faced me.

"Thank you, no," I responded. "I'll run along. I want to tell you, though, little girl, that I am distinctly grateful to you for letting me in on such a nice week of it as I have had."

"The obligation is ours, Richard," said my sister, as she preceded me to the hall. "I don't know what we would have done without you. You helped so much to give them a good time."

She paused with one hand on the doorknob, and turning to me said this:

"Brother, if you were only as good and sensible a man as most people think you are – and as you really are, down deep, where you never have looked at yourself any woman might well be proud of you."

Even Miss Hayden? I wondered if that was in my sister's thought.

CHAPTER VII.

INTROSPECTION

Somewhere I remember reading that every man has three characters, what he is, what he things he is, and what he wants other people to think he is – or something like that, for my quotations are never accurate.

By subdivision it seems to me one may find himself playing a score and more different parts in the course of a day. If I were an author I think I could write a book book, all the characters in which should be drawn from myself – and there would be plenty of them and so various as to be in no danger of recognition as a part and parcel of a single real man.

And which would be the real character? Which would e the real "I"? – I would give a small fortune to find out, to meet him face to face' and to be able to say with confidence, "Now I know myself." If the real "I" was a good sort of a chap that would be desirable. But if not – well, it would be a satisfaction to know it and give up at once the struggle of fighting it.

To little Helen I am a hero – and, lo! with her I feel myself heroic! I act the hero very well, quite unconsciously, for this, audience.

To the Widow I am a man about town, a fellow of the world. A little brighter and smarter than most of the moths that singe themselves at her flame, and so a trifle more desirable for her company. And I feel that I am just a bit brighter and sharper than the majority of fellows.

To Faxon – well, I suppose to ,him I am chiefly a nuisance, and I present as disagreeable a part as I can play when in his company – especially if the Widow is there, and she usually is.

To Gorton Bowie – well, Gorton is a mighty good sort of a chap, and he associates that there is plenty of good in rnr We've been partners for three years, now, ever since the old man died, and I made a stock company of the business and made Bowie treasurer of it. Gorton and I get along very well. Probably each of us supplies something the other lacks. I know he supplies a good deal that I lack – he attends to business and regards me, as he has so often told me, as his kind benefactor who had given him a start in life and done for him more than he could ever repay. When Gorton talks that way I feel as philanthropic as a whole missionary society, and have no further twinges of conscience for letting him do all the work, and find an occasional bit of extra money for me to take a flyer in stocks with.

Ned Marberry, of course, regards me as an irreclaimable fool – and, strangely enough, I feel exactly that way when in his company.

But Kate – ah, dear Kate – you are more charitable. You think I am foolish, but hardly a fool. You look upon me as a man with an unfortunate nature in that, with ample abilities, there is something that prevents them from working out my obvious destiny – which is to amount to something. You upbraid me at one moment and the next you would go through flood and fire for me. You have always had an ideal of me, Kate, and it frets you because I fail to reach the ideal – indeed, if it conies to a crisis you will stand with me against the world and avow that I am, after all, all that you want me to be. With you, Kate, I am a careless, but repentant, boy, whose life is always all before him.

Then there's the Doctor – my dear old yellow-haired Tom! I don't think you ever inspire me to play a part, dear boy. We found each other out pretty thoroughly in the old college days, and if there are any moments in the year when I am neither posing nor imagining, nor feeling, anything but just what I am at those mo-merits, it is when I am with you. You know me better than my own sister possibly better than I know myself. And it is encouraging that you seem to think as much of me to-day as you ever did.

And then there's Mollie Hayden I'd give a world or two to know what you think of me. I was always at my best with you and my best is far from bad, not to sacrifice fact in the interest of unnecessary modesty. Mollie, I think if I were always with you I should be as fine a fellow as there is on earth, and you would never regret – –

Hold on, old man, you are going too fast! You thought that once before. Some one else accepted you at that valuation. The result was what?

Never mind, what. I am a coward when I think of it. I feel as if I were utterly depraved, as thoroughly bad as a man can be, a beast and a brute and yet, that too is but one of the many characters all evolved from the same uneasy soul.

What is a fellow going to do about it? Which one of himself will he settle down with and live with? How is he ever to know which one of him he really is – or, at least, which one comes the closest to meeting the average of them all? Are all men built this way, I wonder? Where am I going to land when all is said and done? Will people speak of me as a brute or a jolly good fellow – or would they speak of me at all?

I suppose environment and circumstance shape the course. Born with the latent seed of a dozen different kinds of fellows within one, environment and circumstance gradually would mould firmly one nature and eliminate the rest until at a sufficient maturity the man comes forth rounded and finished and standing for something.

But. as for me, nearly half the allotted years are gone, and I know not myself. I will not allow that I am a wicked man, and yet I have done some wicked things. I will not allow that I am a stupid man, and yet I have often acted stupidly enough. I cannot claim that I am either good or smart, and yet from time to time my little world has credited me with a plenty of good and smart things. I have a tender heart and my nature is sympathetic; yet I have done one woman a cruel wrong and cannot be sure that I might not repeat the crime should opportunity arise. I would sacrifice my life for a friend like the Doctor or Kate – and yet my friendship is likely to do any of my friends more harm than good before they are done with it. That was the experience of her who was my best friend.

I suppose the trouble is my life has lacked attrition. It has always been too easy. It has permitted the birth of new characters without cultivating, or finishing off, any one of the old original ones, that were perhaps born with me or were evolved in the early days. And now, here I am – a jumble of irreconcilable natures, cast into parts enough for a five-act melodrama – and not knowing whether I'm to be most effective as the hero or the heavy villain, or as the low comedian!

CHAPTER VIII.

DOCTOR TOM

Real life is different from story life, in that there doesn't seem to be any consistent plot to the former.

Real life is a series of incidents usually with only the merest association between them. The culmination of life's story seems usually to be independent of most of the incidents. In story life all the incidents must bear with some closeness on the result, else the story is not a well-told story.

And yet Dr. Tom maintains that even in real life not the smallest episode, incident or thought but that influences its story.

And the story of real life, so the dear old man argues, is the development of a character.

That is all there is to life – so the Doc. talks – to develop character. The working of it out for yourself and the watching of it work out in other persons are, the Doctor claims to think, of more absorbing interest than any romance ever written or any play ever acted.

The subject came up over a pipe and a glass of exceedingly tasty Kirschewasser in the Doctor's quarters, where, on my way to my own rooms, I had dropped in, noting that the midnight incandescent was burning in the little back office.

I had been to the opera with Helen. It was a dangerous experiment, because the chances were good for acquaintances being there who might be curious as to the identity of Helen. As a matter of fact, they were there, plenty of them. The Widow, from two rows in front, faced square about to beam on me, and she leveled her lorgnette on Helen. Gorton Bowie was there, too, with Mrs. Bowie, and I observed that they discussed Helen. Gorton is a good, faithful fellow, as he ought to be, for I have set him up in the world. But his wife, whom he married a few months ago, doesn't regard me highly, and~ apparently thinks neither my business nor any of the rest of the earth could be run without Gorton, and that the universe is indebted ito him accordingly for being alive.

I didn't care anything about the boys. In fact, I was quite glad to have them look at Helen, for she is about as pretty a girl as a fellow could be seen with. I suppose I'll catch it a trifle warmly when I go round to the club, but I can stand it.

I was telling the Doctor about this experience and about Helen, and had remarked how easily a little gossip could be created among one's friends, by appearing in public with a new girl; and, on the other hand, of what infinitesimal importance most of our actions were, anyway.

"Everything spoken by the characters in a book is important, and has an influence on the outcome of the story," I remarked. "In real life, however, our characters chatter away from dawn to dark and it bears on nothing. We do things of importance enough to make interesting chapters for a novel, but they are all disconnected, have no associated purpose, bear upon nothing, and are forgotten – with no possible influence upon the story."

Then the Doctor, pushing his hand through his yellow hair, enunciated the theory about the only plot in life's story being the development of a character, and every trifle must inevitably bear upon that. I had nothing to say to that. When the Doctor gets serious about a thing I never have anything to say.

But I was surprised and not a little startled when the Doctor, after a few puffs of his pipe, turned on me with this:

CONFESSIONS OF A FOOL

"Mind you, Dick, I don't admit that the plot which we demand in our book is altogether absent from real life. For example, yon take this young girl, who is far removed from your circle of acquaintances, and bring her into the full light of their curious gaze in a public place and create your idle, unimportant gossip; what is going to come of it all? Isn't there a chance that a story may after all be opened to be read aye, to the last chapter?"

"Nonsense, Doctor," I returned. "In a book, I suppose you 'mean, I should at this moment properly be the hero of a romance, with Helen as the heroine. Our destinies should work out from our first public appearance to the chancel rail or to a tragic disappointment for one or the other of our parts. And all would live happily, or otherwise, ever after. Now, of course, there is to be nothing of the sort. That is the point I make. With all the talk and gossip among my interested friends that I have created to-night, this chapter in the real life story will amount to nothing. Another chapter will be begun and finished on an entirely irrelevant topic. I will acknowledge that what you call the romance "of the development of a fellow's character may be progressing in proper sequences, but as for the kind of plot in the books, why, Helen is only an inconsequential incident."

The Doctor looked at me sharply for a moment; then he said very slowly:

"My dear Dick, the girl you call Helen may have no place in your story; but did you ever stop to consider that you yourself may be making some mighty important chapters in her romance? For instance, I might ask what you are going to do with this Helen?"

I glared at the Doctor a moment, half inclined to be angry with him. But his lips curled into a smile at the corners, and his mustache twitched mischievously. It is impossible ever to get put out with the Doctor.

"What am I going to do with her!" I echoed. "Why, Tom, I wouldn't harm the girl. Besides, she is quite well able to take care of herself, I assure you. I like her and she likes me. We enjoy being together, and I propose to have her enjoy herself, and to enjoy myself with her."

"Precisely. A perfectly simple exposition. Very natural and as old as the uni verse," said the Doctor. "Not what you would call a Platonic interest, but – – "

"Damn Platonic interest; of course not," I interrupted. "I don't believe there is such a thing. I don't pretend to it, at any rate. I like the girl, like her company; that's all there is about it."

"Just so," said the Doctor, still imperturbable. "You have liked a good many girls before – liked their company. A bright, pretty girl is a pleasant companion, to be sure. It's pleasant to take her around with you, to take her sleigh-riding, and it's fun to hold her little hand in yours and to kiss her – – "

"'Now, Doc, you are laughing at me," I expostulated.

"Never more serious in my life, Dick, although you deserve to be laughed at, sure enough. But it may not be a laughing matter for this unknown Helen, you know. Not that I can have any interest in Helen, or any other girl you may take to, after all, except that in doing her an injury, you do yourself one; and you know I care for you, old man."

"Well, Doc," I ejaculated, "that's a funny way of getting around to me."

"It may be funny, but I would have no reason to interest myself in anybody's affair, except for an interest in one of the parties to it. If I knew Helen I should be inclined to sympathize with her, perhaps. But as it is she is only the indirect cause of my complaint. As I understand it, here is a young girl whose acquaintance you made quite informally, but who, despite that, is an estimable enough young woman, rather beneath you socially and intellectually, I suppose, but bright and amiable enough to be good company. You are not a rake or a roue, and she, as a young business woman, is doubtless very well able to take care of herself if she chooses to. Still the fact that she accepts your attention shows that she likes you fairly well, and, some day, she may think that she is in love with yon. Then what are you going to do about it? Of course you won't be foolish enough to marry her – though you would, if you were the hero of a story, despite friends, social station and everything else. But the last chapter of her story under these circumstances is going to be a pathetic one, and what is to you an incident will be an important part of the plot in her romance, and thus result in some little damage to you as a man. If you should do nothing worse than make a fool of yourself, that's bad enough."

"I don't know why I shouldn't marry Helen," I exclaim, with a spurt of indignation.

"Nonsense!" cried the Doctor, laughing out loud. "You know you would do nothing of the sort. Such an idea would never have entered your head if I hadn't hit you up to it. Don't be any more foolish than you already have been. Only quit your foolishness before you have done any more harm to this girl – and to yourself. You are simply amusing yourself, and you know it. But only fools amuse themselves all the time, and only knaves at other folks' expense."

The Doctor's eyes were quite serious. When I look into those calm eyes of his I am able to see myself much more plainly and clearly than when I face a mirror. I can no more become angry with the reflection than I can when I discover the evidences of a night's spree in the lookingglass the following morning. I take a grim interest in the observation and only want to get away from further contemplation.

We had a good-night heel-tap of the Kirschewasser, and then I departed for my lodgings.

On my dressing-case there is a little framed photograph of Helen. It is a commonplace enough little face there are hundreds like it in the world, no doubt; but the eyes are very bright, the lips halfparted in a smile, a very sweet smile. She is a pretty girl, is Helen.

Perhaps it was the Kirschewasser releasing its delightful hold; perhaps it was a something from what the dear old Doc had said; but as I looked at the picture that night the brightness seemed to go out of Helen's eyes, the smile gave place to a pitiful drooping of the lips.

And then another face seemed to come in the frame. It was the most pitiful face I ever saw. I had known it once, and I often recalled it. A photograph of it lay in a drawer of the dressing-case, and I took it out and looked at it before I retired. It brought the tears to my eyes.

CHAPTER IX.

A DAILY ROUND

I haven't for a long time indulged in the doubtful luxury of a cocktail before breakfast until this morning – after last night's little talk with the Doctor.

I don't believe in the practice, although I used to think it a necessity. This morning, however, I took a cocktail before leaving my rooms for breakfast. I mixed the drink myself, and it was a fine one – as honest as the famous punch that Father Tom concocted for the Pope.

I had not slept very well, but the cocktail had the usual salutary effect, and I felt quite like business when I reached my office. Unfortunately, as I am now disposed to regard it, an old friend and customer from up country dropped in in the forenoon. Gorton Bowie is a good business man for an office, but he doesn't know how to deal with some of our customers. I have to do all the drinking for the concern, and the old friend and I had three or four cocktails before the business transaction that occasioned his visit to town was consummated. After which I lunched him at the club and devoted the afternoon to him up to train time.

The dining hour found me at a favorite cafe, prepared to enjoy a large bottle and a luxurious selection a la carte. The cafe is always lively at this hour, because lots of men and women about town come in for dinner before going to the theatres. The Widow came in, with that confounded Faxon, of course. I had just finished with soup, and I went over to their table to pay my respects to the Widow. She was exceedingly jolly and good natured, patted me on the shoulder and expressed herself as charmed with a "little party she had observed with me at the opera the night before." Was it the same one she had seen me with driving and on the street? How delighted she would be to make her acquaintance. As a friend of mine she was sure the young person would be pleasant to know. Was she an old friend or some one I had but recently met? The latter, of course, else she was sure she would have seen her before. How good of me to pay attention to a young girl scarcely out of her teens. I was always so good. But she trusted I would not forget old friends, etc., etc.

I joined them in a glass of Faxon's sauterne-cup, and the Widow was gracious enough to propose the health of "Dick's unknown."

Then I went back to my dinner, finished my bottle of wine with the fish and had another bottle.

At the theatre a box full of fellows invited me to join them, and proposed that after the last curtain we have a "little game." I invited them to use my rooms and left the theatre just before the curtain rose on the last act, to get things ready and be sure that the tides were not low in the decanters.

I expect the boys every minute. I know what their coming means. They will sit down to play for "just an hour's pastime," and about sunrise they will wind up the pastime with a round of jack-pots. As their host, I shall enjoy having them drink my decanters empty, smoke up the cigars and cigarettes on hand, and probably they will take away with them all the stray cash I have with me.

I face the inevitable with a complacent resignation, born of experience with things inevitable. It will be great fun.

CHAPTER X.

TWO WOMEN AND A MAN

My business trip didn't amount to much, and I didn't dare look Bowie in the face when I came home, lie is such a cautious chap ; never likes to let go of a cent unless he can see a cent and a quarter started and halfway back on the return home to the safe.

Still Bowie is mighty handy. I don't know what I should do without him – don't know what the business would do without him. He keeps a sharp eye on the accounts and collects bills from men that I would rather lose a leg than ask for money. Since we made a stock company of the concern lie has been especially valuable. Doing business as a corporation is very different from a partnership arrangement. He is very proud of his position as treasurer. Just to think of it, it wasn't ten years ago that he came out of college, where he had worked his way to the valedictory, and took a desk in the office at four dollars a week, with his education thrown in. The old man didn't like him at first; took some sort of prejudice against him. But Gorton had so much business sand that the old man had to surrender his prejudices in the face of Gorton's ability. He used to say he wished I was more like Gorton in some respects, and that Gorton was more like me in some respects. Gorton is a little cold, for a fact, and my dear old father liked warm-hearted natures himself – after business hours. He used to say that he liked to see young men have some spirit in their natures – not grow old too fast. But somehow it was the other kind that he took into his employ.

As for Gorton Bowie, he never was cold to me. In fact, when I made stock in the company available to him, no fellow could have exhibited gratitude more warmly. I don't know as I can blame him for being a little stiff sometimes nowadays, for I am aware that I put about as much of the business on his shoulders as he can well stand, and draw out of the treasury about as much money as the business can well stand.

If business wasn't good, however, the trip was not without its advantages. I saw Mollie Hayden. My! what a stunning girl she is. I think she would please even the Doctor. She's what he would call intellectual, even though she doesn't make too obvious a point of it. She told me that Kate had invited her to visit her for a few weeks during Lent, and she thought she would come on. I can't conceive why Kate should arrange for a visit in Lent, when the festivities must of necessity be restricted; but it is fortunate for me, because I shall be able to have more of her company alone and away from the social mob.

Come to think of it, maybe Kate has planned it with that very end in view!

At any rate, I am convinced that I am very much in love. A fellow couldn't make a happier stroke of it than trying to capture Mollie Hayden. A girl like that you wouldn't need to have any sentiment about to be practically happy with. Sentiment is easy enough to arouse in oneself, but solid, substantial happiness is the only real thing worth securing, or that you can get any sort of a firm grip on.

I wonder what Helen will have to say should I ever tell her that I hope to be married. I don't natter myself that she will take it much to heart, for she is a very business-like little party, and decidedly matter-of-fact. I have got in the habit recently of making quite a confidante of Helen. As a confidante she is delightful. Eminently sympathetic, yet without much nonsense in her composition. She told me she thought it very foolish to sell stock in my business so to get funds for outside investment, as I did last January. That was quite a wise opinion, and shows what a common-sense sort of a head Helen has on her shoulders, though I silenced her when I told her about the snug little profit I secured from the spec. We had a little supper on it, and Helen sipped a glass of champagne. The charming girl was altogether sweet.

It seems queer, when I stop to think about it, this habit I have got into of telling Helen all sorts of things about myself. She never has anything to say about herself now, but seems wonderfully interested in what concerns me, whether it be business or pleasure. I really do not think I could ever talk over my own affairs with any other woman alive – not even Mollie Hayden. And I enjoy it immensely with Helen. If s a relief when I'm worried to talk with her, and it is a pleasure had over again to recite my good times to her.

Some day you'll fall in love with some fine fellow, Helen, and marry him. And I will be your godfather and see that you have something handsome to remind you of the days when we were chums.

CHAPTER XI.

THE UNEXPECTED

Mollie Hayden looked inexpressibly fine when she stepped off the train, and she greeted me with as delicious a smile as it was ever my good fortune to get.

She rode up to the house with us – Kate and I. The two girls – I shall always call Kate a girl, I suppose, though she's thirtyeight, if she's a day – sat on the back seat, and I was with the man in front. Marberry has recently acquired a man, and is altogether cutting quite a wide swathe as he grows older. I am glad he is doing so well, for Kate's sake.

Mollie chatted about the trip, and Kate and I were good listeners. Mollie's voice is, as I think I have before observed, a distinct contralto, quite heavy, but 'wonderfully good-toned and resonant. Cultivated, I think she could sing like Scalchi in her best days. Her enunciation is altogether delightful. I believe she has had some dramatic training. She says "won't" and not "woon't" and never permits the final "t" and the following "y" to make "chew" when she says "won't you."

I left the Marberrys early after dinner with a promise to call the next forenoon, and proceed to make myself entertaining. The snow is all off the ground, though not out of it, and the early Spring days are beginning to be comfortable for outof-doors diversion. We found that Mollie had no objections to a Lenten theatre party, and I agreed to help Kate in making up one before the week was out. Kate had already planned a mild and unsacrilegions reception and an afternoon tea, and these were expected to open the doors for a return of courtesies of a similarly harmless nature to help to make Mollie's Lenten visit pleasant, if not hilarious.

I asked permission to bring the Doctor to luncheon next day. To tell the truth, I wanted to shoulder onto the Doctor some of the pleasant burden of helping Kate out. The Doctor is full of expedients and can think up unique ideas for entertaining a woman far better than I ever could. If Mollie were a man, I would be more at home at devising entertainments. Indeed, I have quite a reputation in that line, and am quoted abroad as a vender of good times on so splendid a scale that the recipients do not recover from them for some days after they get out of town, and hold them in tender memory until they may, happily, return for more.

I never knew the Doctor to exhibit himself more charmingly than he did at luncheon. He quite let himself loose to be agreeable to Kate, and seemed to enjoy immensely Mollie's vigorous attempts to combat him over certain questions affecting woman's sphere, which came up for 'cross-the-table discussion. The Doctor elucidated some pronounced ideas as to the sphere of woman, which developed the fact that Miss Hayden had equally pronounced ideas of her own and quite seriously in opposition to those held by the Doctor. Before the dispute, the Doctor rather staggered me by wanting to know if Miss Hayden wouldn't enjoy going through one of the hospitals, a suggestion which the superb young woman seized upon with a cheerful alacrity. So we planned to all visit the hospital next day.

Mollie Hayden in a hospital seemed quite as much at home as Mollie Hayden in a drawing-room, and expressed a little astonishment that, intimately acquainted as we were with a house surgeon, Kate and I had heretofore neglected to take advantage of it in this wise. It appeared that our guest, while possessed of no superior knowledge of medicine and surgery, knew the difference between a deltoid muscle and a corpuscle, and proved a most intelligent listener to what the Doctor had to say to her. The two women had brought some flowers for distribution among the sufferers, and the experience was altogether pleasant and not unprofitable.

I remarked to Kate as we watched the Doctor explaining to Miss Hayden some sort of a mechanism for the convenient repose of a broken leg, that I thought, if my yellow-headed friend could find another woman like Mollie Hayden, he would cease to be so generally benevolent in his associations with womankind, and make up his mind to marry that particular one.

Indeed, I repeated that remark in substance to Doctor Tom one evening some weeks later, as Miss Hayden's stay was drawing to a close. The Doctor and I were driving home in the former's buggy from the Marberrys' after an evening of progressive euchre – a pastime that is despicable to my mind, and fitted only for Lenten makeshift. The Doctor whipped up his horse, and remarked that he didn't believe there was another woman on earth like Miss Hayden. There was so extraordinary a tone in his voice, and the words echoed what was in my own mind so exactly, that my cigar nearly slipped from between my fingers.

"Come in," said the Doctor, as he turned the hitch-up over to his boy at the office door. We went into the cosy rooms, where my good friend receives patients who are able to be out, and he arranged a pair of leather-covered easy chairs in front of the open hearth, and proceeded to poke a smouldering log into flame, for the Spring dampness still kept the office chilly.

"What'll you have?" inquired the Doctor, sententiously, as I dropped into one of the leather chairs, while he stood by the other, awaiting my pleasure.

"Nothing better than whiskey at this hour," I remarked, modestly.

The Doctor plunged his hands into his pockets and looked intently into the fire, as if for the moment he had forgotten his immediate surroundings and was allowing his mind to wander in even pleasanter paths. He awakened with a start.

"Whiskey, did you say?" he cried out, with a peculiar thrill in his voice. "Nonsense, old man; that is dross. I have a case of Imperial Cuvee that one of my patients presented me only last week, which I believe was built for this occasion. Finish your cigar while I fetch up a quart."

"And whit is this especial occasion?" I inquired, as the Doctor returns with the handsome package of sparkling wine, a couple of glasses, and a bowl of ice, for the latter of which he apologizes.

"I hadn't opened the case," he explains, "and. you will have to use the ice in your glass. What is the especial occasion, do you ask?" and the Doctor snapped the stout cord of wire about the neck of the bottle, and with his strong-tipped fingers, proceeded to work at the cork to start it. "Well, I'm going to be married to a lovely woman. As my oldest and nearest friend, I give you the earliest authoritative information, and ask you to quaff a little of this fine wine to our health and happiness."

"And the wedding is to come off when?" I inquire, quite calmly.

"Some time in the Fall."

"And the lovely woman is who?"

"Miss Hayden," and "pop!" went the champagne cork toward the ceiling.

I rise from the big chair and shake the Doctor's hand warmly. Then he fills the glasses, touching them together with a hearty clink, as in the old college days. We sip off the topmost beads, and as the Doctor places the bottle on the floor between us, we both sit down. The logs on the hearth crackle, and I am watching the flame. The Doctor is watching me with the smile of a boy, his blue eyes sparkling. After a moment, I remarked with a laugh:

"Doctor, you are a rapid worker when you undertake a case."

"Well, Dick," said he, "I don't believe there is anybody so charming in the world as this friend of your sister's, Marberry's cousin. To see her was to admire her, and to know her was to love her beyond measure. To be sure, the acquaintance has been only a short one, but it seems as if I had known her a lifetime. I made up my mind before I was thirty that I should never marry. My profession had for me all the interest I wanted in life. But, when I woke up and realized that that girl's face was before my eyes day and night, I came to the conclusion that I needed her, and decided that I would have her if I could get her. I've built up a good practice, my income is sufficient, and I don't, see why I shouldn't have what I want."

"Strikes me you were a little precipitate. Doc," I suggest, with an attempt of playful criticism.

"And why not?" demanded the Doctor, quite seriously. "The risk of venturing to ask her was all mine, and when I look back upon it, I realize that it was a tremendous risk, for I have been little more than ordinarily attentive to her since she has been here – since I have known her. I suppose the wiser plan is to do your courting first, but as I have had neither a desire to, nor experience in, paying court, 1 neglected to go at it that way. Fortunately it has come out all right, and I can do my courting now.

"It's a delicate subject, Doctor," I remark, after a few more sips of the wine, "but the situation is so peculiar, that I would like immensely to know how Miss Hayden accepted it."

The Doctor laughs pleasantly, and replies: "Why, I would as lief tell you as not, but I don't know. I remember asking her if she would be my wife, or something to that effect, and then I remember thinking that I ought to say something about being in love with her. But somehow that wouldn't come. I think she said nothing whatever, except 'yes,' and I remember that she said it in a very clear voice, quietly enough. And that is all there was to it. It was a very simple operation, after all."

Neither of us speaks for a few moments. Then the Doctor picks the bottle from the floor and passes it to me with:

"Here; finish this wine. I shan't want another drop. It somehow tastes as flat as water."

And I finish the quart. It tasted like fire to me glorious fire. I wanted fire.

CHAPTER XII.

JUST DYSPEPSIA

What the novelists call a disappointment in love affects a man differently at different periods of life.

If he is twenty-one it comes as near to breaking his heart as that operation is possible of accomplishment.

At twenty-six it may drive him to drink.

After he has passed thirty the result is likely to be an attack of nervous dyspepsia.

And from a somewhat satisfying experience I have come to the conclusion that nervous dyspepsia is by all odds the worst infliction that it lies within the power of woman to impose upon a man.

And yet, I haven't the heart to throw any blame upon Miss Hayden. Indeed, I am compelled to a respect that almost overcomes the sentiments of admiration with which she always inspired me, because, knowing so little about me, she yet instinctively realized that I am not the best fellow in the world for her if, indeed, I am for any one.

The Widow, to be sure, assures me that I am the best fellow in the world for anybody, although she does not hesitate to avail herself of Faxon's trap, or yacht, even though I may not be present, and when, indeed, I would be pleased to place at her disposal my modest Goddard, with myself for her sole companion.

Kate was very much disturbed when next I called upon her, which was several days after the enjoyment of the Doctor's quart bottle. I dropped in after the lunch eon hour, and learned that Miss Hay den was out – with the Doctor. Kate in formed me that the Doctor had been very attentive to her guest, as well as to herself, in my absence, and her voice expressed something much like disappointment.

"Of course you know the reason, Kate," I ventured.

"Mollie has told me everything," replied my sister. "Your friend, the Doctor, is a very charming fellow, but I hoped for something different."

"For my sake, I know you mean, Kate," I said. "Well, I can but feel that Miss Hayden is altogether too splendid a woman to be used as a redeemer for a fellow like me."

"You are unjust to yourself, Dick," said my sister. "You are well connected and generally well regarded. You are weak and careless with yourself, but – – " and Kate paused.

"But very few persons have tumbled to the fact yet – that's what you would say?" I suggest, with desperate flippancy.

"Perhaps that is what I mean, and perhaps it is not," returned my sister, with some severity. "You mustn't talk about yourself in that style – you mustn't think about yourself in that way. You are kind and good and clever with the rest of the world, and it's time you had some respect for yourself. If you would marry some good woman she could make you respect yourself. Indeed, if you could have won a girl like Mollie Hayden, that alone could but raise you in your own estimation to a proper regard for yourself."

"Precisely – and I find that I simply can't fool that kind of woman," I remark, with an ugly laugh.

"What a wretched state you are in," cried Kate, angrily. "I don't ask you to fool anybody. I only want you to be yourself – your better self. Any woman would be proud to be my brother's wife if he were only as much of a man as he might be, and you know it."

"Humph! That's like regretting that the talents possessed by a first-class burglar or murderer were not turned into more respectable directions when we know that, however clever the talents are, they would have been flat and unproductive if they hadn't been occupied according to their bent – burgling or murdering. A smart mechanic wouldn't necessarily make a smart preacher. You can't tune the catgut of your guitar to sound like the wire string, although it may be the finest piece of catgut in the world. I can't be any different than I am, Kate, and, to tell the truth, I've about given up trying."

"That's a man's sophistry," cried Kate, with decision. Her eyes flashed and her bosom rose and fell with quick, angry breaths. "Decent influences could make up for the qualities that are lacking in you to make you as fine a man as there is in the world. Miss Hayden could have done it."

"And you would have risked sacrificing her to the undertaking. That's very good of you, Kate."

"I would sacrifice myself for you, Dick. But I don't think she would have been sacrificed."

"One woman tried it and failed," I remark, after a moment.

"Yes, poor little thing. But you were younger, then, and she was hardly the kind of a girl to save a man, sweet and dear as she was."

"I would give a good deal to have her back again," I interrupt, with bitterness.

"Of course you would, dear," said my sister, tenderly. "Of course you would. And I feel that you owe to her a great deal as it is, and that we all do."

"It cost her too much," I put in savagely. "I don't want to talk about it. I wish she and you had let me alone to tumble into a dissolute's grave ten years ago."

"Oh, Dick!" pleaded my sister. "Don't talk so. You make me sick at heart. I only mean this, if she had been a stronger woman, stronger in will and in body, and yet possessed of all her sweetness and graciousness, she would have accomplished what her love for you inspired her to set out to do."

"Precisely, Kate, but the women of the kind you mention have too fine a destiny to pursue and too noble a sphere to fill to make sacrifices for the sake of redeeming some damn fool who, when he is redeemed, may prove not to be worth the bother."

"Well, Dick," said my sister, after looking at me intently for a moment that seemed like an hour, "I don't know as I know what anybody is going to do for you, or do with you, when you talk and feel like that. I only know this, that the love of a good and a strong and high-minded woman is powerful to inspire a man to think well of himself, and I don't know of anything else that is so powerful. Miss Hayden is that kind of a woman. I tell you frankly, what you already know, that I wanted you to marry her. I was willing to commit myself to the effort to bring it about – for your sake, and because, too, I did not fear that you would fail me or ever make her or me regret it. That is all over now, Dick. I don't know how you feel about it, but you are a man and not a boy, and will the more readily feel assured that there are other women in the world as good, as brilliant, as attractive, as Mollie Hayden. I wish you would find such a one and induce her to be your wife."

"The expediency of following your suggestion is unquestionable," I remark, with an attempt at a laugh. "And, perhaps, when I am a little bit older, love will more readily wait upon expediency."

Kate's eyes were moist, but she was evidently quite glad to have me laugh at her a little.

You may be as mischievous with me as you like, Dick," she returned, with a smiling light drying up the moisture in her eyes. "Only try and be true to yourself."

CHAPTER XIII.

HOT AND THIRSTY DAYS

I think this has been the most dismal summer I ever passed in my life. I have been in town through all the hot days, and have haunted the clubs day and night for company. The Marberrys' house has been closed, and the Doctor was away during August, spending a part of the time, I understand, at the Hayden's. I haven't seen him, and don't want to see him or, anybody else but the circle of good fellows who meet in the early evenings after dinner at the Claremont, and, sitting in the cool of the club windows, sip endless mixtures until the club lights are extinguished. The days following are often passed in a measure of mental and physical misery, redeemed by a Turkish bath in the afternoon and the inevitable cocktail before dinner and the Claremont cocktail is of a character to change the whole face of nature and make the .hot city pavements to seem to blossom with roses and chrysanthemums. They are wonderfully comforting, too, when the stock market has been raising the devil with my margins.

Thank Heaven, Gorton Bowie likes to attend to business. There hasn't been much business to attend to, to be sure, but what there is commands his entire effort. His family is in the country, and he runs down every night. He has occasionally invited me to put in a Sunday with him, but I despise the country, and, moreover, as social creatures, neither Bowie nor his wife is compatible – hardly bearable. Indeed, since I turned over to him that last block of our company's stock to get a small loan to help me with my investments, I am disposed to see as little of him as is necessary. I don't know where Bowie gets all his money, but he is always ready to advance me reasonable sums. He has ever been a saving sort of a soul, and I am credibly informed that small savings accumulate into sizable deposits if they are kept up long enough.

If there has been one ray of white light in this – to look back upon it – dark summer it has been. Helen. I have taken Helen over a number of pretty drives and on an excursion or two, and we have visited the parks and the summer gardens together. Helen's mother has accompanied us on some of these. Helen's mother is an invalid, and I have learned that Helen is not only her sole support, but that the girl is practically compelled to support that rapscallion of a brother of hers. Helen is delightful company, always. I find that she has read some good books that I used to read in my college days, and I undertook to look some of them over so that we might have them for a subject of conversation.

I wonder what Kate would say to Helen?

CHAPTER XIV.

HELEN

I want to jot down right here a little incident while it is fresh in my mind. It relates to Helen. A good many of my thoughts recently have had relation to Helen. I don't know, now, which way I shall direct them, after what has happened.

It was the night of the wedding Miss Hayden and the Doctor. Of course, I was best man. It is not unusual for the groom to make a best man of the fellow who most wanted to be himself groom, although I don't think either the Doctor or Miss Hayden ever regarded me seriously as such a possibility.

The wedding was at high noon, in church, with a reception at the home of the bride's parents. Later in the afternoon bride and groom departed on their wedding journey. I left the company in the reception room, and, lighting a cigar, strolled out on the lawn to breathe the cool October breezes. While occupied with a miscellaneous collection of thoughts inspired by the event of the day and the cigar, a servant brought me a telegram. I opened it and read the following message:

"Mother is dead. Can you come to me?

"HELEN."

There was something in those five last words that made my heart leap. It had been many years since I had realized the deliciousness of having some one – some woman – depend upon me for anything.

Helen and I had never exchanged a written word in the course of our acquaintanceship. The simple confidence expressed in that telegraphed query, "Can you come to me?" was positively delightful.

I left the hospitable home of the Haydens that night. The next evening found me in the house of mourning. Neighbors had been in and had helped Helen in her extremity. The rapscallion brother was away, no one knew where. Drunk, probably. Helen's mother had died very suddenly, passing away while asleep in her chair. Helen was overcome with grief and the loneliness and helplessness of her position, and when she let me in at the door she burst into tears. I took her hand and she led me into the little parlor.

Helen

"You were good to come – I didn't know what to do – the people about me have been very kind – but somehow I needed some one stronger – I wanted you and you were away I couldn't help asking you – and, oh! you are so good to come – – " she tried to explain in broken sentences.

I calmed her as well as I knew how. As a rule, houses of mourning are not congenial to me, as they are quite unfamiliar. My mother died when I was too young to appreciate her loss, and my father's passing away seemed so much a matter of course that it did not impress me except as the departure forever from my side of a true and good friend. I have always felt a sort of cowardly desire to shun pain and suffering and let unhappiness and grief take care of themselves.

Somehow, though, I was conscious of a certain unharmonious pleasure sitting here with Helen as her main dependence in her hour of unparalleled distress.

All this only leads up to the incident I started to jot down. Helen's troubles did not end with the funeral. By her mother's death she came into ownership of the little cottage, but living there was dreadfully lonesome for her, I knew. I suggested that she might find some girl among her acquaintances with whom she might keep house, but it appeared that Helen had very few acquaintances, and none that was available for such a co-partnership. It was an evident wrong to her to have her keep the cottage open for her miserable brother's sake, and finally one night after Christmas I jumped into another solution of her unfortunate problem.

We had been sleigh-riding. It was the first outing Helen had allowed herself to take since the mother's death. We returned to the cottage before ten o'clock, and I went in with her. She looked wonderfully pretty after the brisk ride. Her cheeks were red and her gray eyes shone. I asked her to play for me, and while she sat at the piano I stepped up behind her and put my arms about her shoulders, clasping my hands together tightly. She stopped playing and her hands went up to mine as if to unclasp them. But she did not unclasp them, but let her own hands rest on them, and her head dropped forward a little.

"Helen," I said, hardly able to raise my voice above a whisper, "suppose I should tell you that I loved you?"

The little woman didn't speak for a long minute. Then she unclasped my hands and gently lifting my arms from about her shoulders, wheeled slowly about on the piano stool until she faced me standing before her. She had not released my hands from hers, and she looked straight up into my eyes.

Helen

"Do you want to tell me that?" she asked, quite soberly.'

"To tell the truth, Helen," I replied, with a little laugh at her unexpected question, "I feel decidedly like it to-night. May I tell you?"

"Do you love me?" she returned, still looking straight into my eyes.

I looked down into the pupils with their disc of gray, and then I raised her from the piano stool and led her to a big easy chair across the room. I drew one of the dignified little chairs that always adorn the humblest parlor to the side of hers and sat down in it.

After a while I spoke to her.

"Helen," said I, "you and I are exceedingly good friends, are we not?"

"I hope so you have been very kind to me."

"I am alone in the world you are alone in the world. We seem to like each other. I have sometimes thought I loved you. I think I am sure of it to-night, dear."

Helen didn't speak. She turned her eyes from me, and clasping her hands in her lap allowed her head to fall back against the heavy upholstery of the chair. Then her eyes closed.

"Are you sure you don't pity me and think that is love?" she said, softly, her eyes opening and regarding me a little curiously, although they were moist, and something like a tear-drop glistened on the lower lids.

"To be honest with you, then, dear," I replied, "if you will have it so, I cannot tell you. I don't know. I do know that love is inspired by a great variety of emotions. I have thought myself in love before nowmost fellows do before they reach my age."

"And what, may I ask what emotions have made you love before?"

I looked at Helen somewhat startled, and wondering if she were quizzing me. She certainly was not. Her voice was very gentle, and she was still regarding me with half-opened eyes. There was more moisture in them.

"Well," I replied, "I once loved a woman because I was confident she loved me."

"And how did that turn out?"

"I don't know as I care to tell even you, Helen not now, dear. But not happily for the girl, who really did love me more than I ever expect to be loved again."

"Was not that what was to have been expected?"

"I understand it now, Helen, but I was perhaps too young a fellow to discover it then in time until it was too late."

Helen

"Then you were married?" said Helen, almost in a whisper.

"Yes."

Helen's eyes closed again and neither of us spoke for a little while. Finally Helen said, her eyes still closed.

"And how about the next one?"

"Well, there wasn't any next one for a long time. I had very little of woman's company for what seemed like a great many years. The only 'next one' there was was a beautiful girl whom any man would admire, and I believe most any man fall in love with without much trouble."

"And you fell in love with her?"

"I suppose I did, in a way. I really didn't have a chance to find out. Besides, I had come across you, Helen, in the mean time."

Helen's lips trembled into a smile, a pretty smile, a dainty smile, as sweet a smile as I had ever seen. Her eyes opened, her face flushed slightly, and she raised her head and looked again straight at me. My hands were grasping the arm of her chair, and she placed both her own over them.

"Does anybody – any young woman, I mean, call you by your first name?" she demanded, suddenly.

"Only my sister."

"And your sister is nice, isn't she if she is like you? And there is no one else?"

"Not a soul, that I know of now." I forgot the Widow, but she does not count.

"Then I am going to. I'm going to call you 'Dick.' Now, my dear Dick," said Helen, suddenly, "what would your sister say if she knew you were here with me and had told me you loved me?"

What a queer question that seemed.

"Why, Helen," I exclaimed, "I'm sure, if she knew you, she could but be pleased."

"Is she older or younger than you?"

"Older, and married."

"And thinks a great deal of you, of course. Did you ever speak to her of me?"

I was quite staggered at this, and could only reply with ill-concealed embarrassment that I had never thought to speak of Helen to Kate.

"Precisely," said this strangely matterof-fact little woman. "Now, don't think me unkind, and don't reply to me if I say that you did not regard acquaintance with me as of sufficient account to mention it to your sister. I think a great deal of you, Dick – how could I do otherwise when you have been so good to me? You have been a real friend, and real friends are rare for a girl in my position to find among men."

"Don't talk like that, Helen," I expostulated. "What difference does it make about a woman's position if she is only a good woman? No man could be otherwise than good to you."

"It makes a great deal of difference – and you know it does. Now let me tell you something. I have worked for my living ever since I came out of high school when my father died. I have been thrown constantly among men, and I never saw a man, before I met you, that was not disposed to take advantage of a return of his friendliness. And then he behaved foolishly. I learned, early enough, that a woman in business must confine herself strictly to business if she would save herself from annoyance from her fellows, the men, who were in business. I read a great deal about the freedom of the field of professions and business open to women, but I found out that if a woman, a young and fairly attractive woman, is going to pursue them, she must debar herself from those little attentions which a girl likes to receive from men, when they are offered by men in her business circle or who enter it to seek her. Since I have known you I have felt perfectly free with you – always at ease and ready to go with you anywhere. I have had more pleasant hours with you than I ever had with any one in all my life. You have never offered to kiss me – you have never been foolish. When the occasion came that I needed you for something beside a good time you came to me; and, if I had not known before how real a friend you were, I discovered it then. I respect you and I like you, and I am glad you like me – I know you do, or you would not have been so kind to me in so many ways."

Helen's eyes were filled with tears, now, and as she stopped speaking she bent over and her head fell forward on her hands, clasping mine on the arm of the chair. I raised my disengaged hand and stroked her hair. I wanted to kiss her hair.

"Well, Helen," said I, after a while, "what does all this amount to, dear? Do you mean that it is foolish for me to tell you that I love you? That certainly isn't kind to me, Helen."

"I don't know whether it is or not," responded the girl, raising her head and looking at me intently. "I don't know whether it is foolish or not. I know you are impetuous. I know you are the kind of a man who wouldn't do a wrong thing, or a foolish thing, if you took time to consider it but you might do a great many such because you

Helen

would not take time to consider. You remember when you first took me home from that ball – when you threw that fellow into the street. To tell the truth, I was more afraid of you, for a moment, than I was of the fellow you threw into the street. I could have taken care of the situation unaided. But I liked yon when you stepped up to protect me. I had not for a long time felt the need of a protector, or ever looked for one. It was pleasant to have one, and I was afraid, before we parted, you would do or say something foolish to spoil it all. And when you did not, I liked it and liked you and wanted to see you again," and Helen laughed out loud as if she were happy.

I laughed, too, at the recollection of the incident. Then I said:

"And how about now, dear?"

"Well," returned Helen, speaking very slowly, "I don't know how to say it to you, but I wish you wouldn't speak any more about it not to-night, at least. Believe me, I am thinking of you of your interests – – "

"But don't do it, Helen!" I interrupted. "I am perfectly able to take care of myself. I know exactly what I am about. If a man loves a woman why shouldn't he be permitted to tell her so? If she is a good woman her love is an honor to him."

"That is very nice to say," returned Helen, shaking her head and smiling at me. "The novel writers always put it that way, Dick. But you know, 'way down deep, that there are other considerations and," with a mischievous laugh, "I'm not at all certain that men know what they are about even when they think they do."

I had nothing to say to that, and after a pause, Helen spoke again:

"Now let me ask you to do something more for me." And the girl raised herself erect and took her hands from off mine. "Please forget that you have told me that you loved me. Please remember, if you wish it, that you have asked me if you might love me. I know you like me, and I am afraid you pity me. Now, I want you to think things over – a lot of things. I want you to tell your sister about me. I should like to meet your sister. Call on me when you please as you have always done. Invite me to ride or to walk with you, or to the theater, whenever it will be pleasant for you to have me with you. I have arranged to rent the cottage to a nice family and to board with them, and you may come here as often as you wish to. Now," and Helen drew a little watch from her waist, "you see it is after eleven o'clock. You must be going. But before you go, I will play and sing one song for you."

Helen

Helen rose quickly from her chair. I rose, too, and seized both her hands in mine. Then I bent slowly and kissed her on the cheek. She laughed a sweet, low laugh, with something like sadness in it.

"Helen," said I, "you are the dearest girl in the world."

She looked smilingly at me, but made no answer.

CHAPTER XV.

GORTON BOWIE

"You have overdrawn your account by nearly a thousand dollars, sir. I would suggest that you refrain from drawing any more."

I looked at Gorton Bowie with some dismay. I needed money not much, but enough to save my margins. They had all but been wiped out by the day's operations, and my brokers assured me that my stocks would be pretty sure to drop another halfpoint on the morrow.

"What do you mean, Bowie?" I demanded. "That I can't take money from iny own safe?"

"I mean this, sir – – " Gorton Bowie always addressed me as "sir," he had never called me by my Christian name, and only rarely by my surname; then with a "Mr." before it. I know of no other acquaintance, of many months' standing, who does not know me with the easy familiarity of "Dick" "I only mean this, sir; that there aren't sufficient funds in the drawer to supply you, and I must respectfully decline to sign a check."

"But, Bowie," I expostulated. "What does this mean?"

"Nothing more than what I say, sir. We have no money to spare and you are already overdrawn."

"No money to spare! Shall we not be able to declare a dividend at the annual meeting day after to-morrow?"

"We certainly shall not be able to. I must remind you that business has been far from healthy the past six months."

"Well, you have been managing it," I retorted, as a vent to my angry feelings.

"Exactly – and if I had not managed it, it would have been worse," returned Bowie, calmly eyeing me.

"That's right, Bowie, that's right," I acknowledged, relenting a little. "I have thrown a pretty heavy burden on you the past year or two. But I don't take kindly to being held up in this way – and I don't feel disposed to transfer any more of my stock to you and borrow money. But I must have funds, and I must have them by to-morrow morning, the first thing."

"You can't have them out of this business, sir," Bowie remarked, with calm decision.

CONFESSIONS OF A FOOL

"I can't have them!" I repeated after him, astonished at the flatness of his refusal. "Do you mean to say I can't have them?"

"That is exactly what I mean, sir." Bowie was appallingly calm and precise. He always is. "You forget, sir, that I own a majority of this stock."

I felt a strange coldness pass all over me as if I had suddenly plunged into a needle bath that ran ice water. For a moment I could not find my voice.

Forget it! I had never thought of it! And yet I knew it well enough – knew that I had borrowed money from Bowie and had given him my stock as collateral until he had in his possession nearly two-thirds of all the stock of the concern, properly transferred and all his as far as the papers showed.

"But that stock is mine – when I choose to buy it back," I finally gasped.

"Precisely – when you choose to buy it

back," responded Bowie, deliberately. "When you do choose to buy it back, it will be time to talk about it. It is in my possession now and it is mine."

"But – but – " I ejaculated, hardly knowing how to face the situation, "you do not propose to – to – use it – and against me?"

Gorton Bowie

"What I propose to do will appear at the proper time," said Bowie, still unflinchingly calm. "I don't care to loan you any more money on any more of your stock, though. I have quite enough of it now," and a disagreeable smile played at the corners of his thin lips.

I looked hard at him for a moment. His face was very white, his lips tightly compressed. He looked mean and cowardly but nervy. I had it in my mind to seize him by the throat and wring his neck.

"Gorton Bowie," I exclaimed, at last. "I believe you are planning to play me a dirty trick."

Bowie merely bowed his head exasperatingly, as if waiting for me to say more that was abusive.

"If you do," I cried, my hands clinching, "I will make you suffer for it. You are a miserable dog. I have placed you where you are and made you what you are. You can keep the stock and take this business from me, but, by God, I'll thrash you till you won't walk for a week if you play with me this way."

Gorton Bowie looked me squarely in the eye and then his eyes dropped and he turned to his desk. It was early evening and not a soul was in the place but we two. The office door was closed. In my rising anger I itched to jump upon him. Ho could have had the balance of my interest for that satisfaction. I glared at him and probably looked to him as much like a wild beast as I felt.

"I propose to be able to defend myself,'* said Bowie, with a little wavering of his voice.

"What do you mean by that?" I demanded, stepping nearer to him.

He jumped back with an expression of fear in his thin face, as if he thought I was preparing to strike him. I had no such intention, though I was angry enough to do it, and I probably showed it. lie reached his arm back, opened a drawer in his desk, and, the next thing I knew, I saw the nickel of a revolver flashing in his hand.

In the state of mind I was in that gleaming nickel was enough to knock the last bit of self-control out of my head. I rushed at him and made a kick at his hand with my right foot. It was a trick I had learned from a French boxer in Paris. My foot struck his knuckles with a thump. He gave a cry of pain and the revolver went flying into the air, landing on a table halfway across the room.

I stepped to the table, and picking the weapon up, handed it back to him. My rage had begun to cool.

"There!" I cried. "Put that thing away. You are too mean to strike. But if you ever attempt that sort of a trick again I'll thrash you till you can't walk."

Gorton Bowie

I recalled to myself the remark of Roscoe Conkling on a memorable occasion, when he pointed out that while a man should be careful in his associates, he should be choice in his fighting. And I regarded Bowie, as he put back the revolver in the drawer, with a feeling of satisfaction that I had refrained from half -killing him.

Bowie crossed the room and proceeded to put on his hat and overcoat. He closed his desk, and saying "Goodnight" without looking at me again, left the office.

I heard him pass down the stairs and out of the building, and then I ant down at mv own desk and began to think.

My thoughts are not worth recording, even for my own future reference. They were dismal – pitiable.

Once I spoke out loud. I said:

"Dick, old man, you have been a fool!"

CHAPTER XVI.

THE RELIEF
OF CONFESSION

"Dick!" exclaimed my sister, a few days after the disturbing scene recorded in my last memoranda. "What was the meaning of that paragraph I saw in the paper yesterday morning?"

She was advancing into the reception room to greet me. Her right hand was extended, and I took it and held on to it.

I knew well enough to what particular paragraph she referred. It was a brief notice to the effect that the management of the old house which bore my father's name in its corporate title had undergone a change 'by the retirement of the senior partner – myself. It stated further that the business would be carried on under the same name, but that Mr. Gorton Bowie, its treasurer since the company was organized, had succeeded to the presidency, still holding his former office, and would be the controlling power and active manager of the concern in the future.

"It means just what it says, Kate," I replied. "I have sold out to Bowie."

"Sold out to Bowie!" cried my sister. "What do you mean? Do you mean to tell me that you have sold out your interest in our father's business?"

"Well, no, not sold it out entirely. But enough of it to place the control in other hands. I still own some stock there, but shall take no active part in the concern in the future."

Kate looked stern, and her pretty mouth was closed tightly. She gazed so hard at me that despite myself I could not look back at her.

"Dick," she said, in a hard voice, "you have done some wrong. I know you have. Something has happened that you have never told me about."

I made no response.

"Dick," she went on, "you must tell me. I must know. What is the matter a man of your years doesn't 'retire from business,' from a good business, unless there is an extraordinary reason for it. What is the matter? Has the business run down?"

"No – the business is all right, I think. But I have run down," I cried out desperately. "I suppose I have run down, Kate."

"You suppose you have?" echoed my sister, her voice sounding very harsh and even disagreeable. "What do you mean by that, Dick?"

I looked down at her hand, still held in mine, pushed the rings around her fingers, and then, feeling like a boy who expects to get a spanking promptly on confession, looked up at her and said:

"Kate, to be honest, I suppose I am about ruined in a business way."

There was a queer sound in the woman's throat. She turned very white, then red again. Her eyes flashed, her lips twitched. And then, the eyes filled with tears. She spoke softly, very softly:

"Dick, my brother, what has brought this about?"

I had no mind to keep anything back. I wanted a confidante. I was ashamed to make use of one. I did not want Helen to know, sweet as she is. I would tell my sister.

"Speculation, I suppose, Kate," I said, "outside investments, I prefer to call it. That is at the bottom of it. I have lost a great deal of money the past eighteen months. Have lost more than I have had to lose. Now I've lost my business. I have nothing left – except some stock in the company, which will give me an income according to the amount of profits. Not enough to live on – for me to live on."

We sat down together on the lounge and I told her the whole wretched story. I had not comprehended how wretched a story it was until this moment when I began to put it into words.

"But, Dick," Kate interrupted, once, "was there no one to help you out of such a situation could you not have borrowed money to have bought back that stock?"

"Well, Kate," I said, "I might have done it, though it was pretty late to try before I realized how near to the brink I was. And, Kate, my intimates are not of the class of men who have much money to loan. They are too good fellows to have any spare cash on hand," and I laughed.

"Good fellows will ruin you," said my sister. "Good fellows ruin themselves. You have ruined yourself. But I should think there would have been business acquaintances who could have been approached."

"Maybe so, but I am afraid that my credit was not so good among business acquaintances as it is among the good fellows who had no money to lend me."

"You might have asked me, Dick," said my sister, after a pause. "I could have secured enough from my own funds to have bought back your stock."

"Yes, Kate, I know you would wipe out your box at the deposit company for me, but nothing in my character or past career justifies me in calling upon my dear sister to bank anything on my future."

"Is it too late to recover your interest in the business?" she asked, after the story was all told.

"I suppose not – but it calls for more money than I am likely to see for some time. I think I could compel Bowie to sell me back my stock – or lick him," I added, with a laugh, for I had got over being ugly with Bowie, or anybody else even with myself.

Kate had nothing more to say, and I was glad to drop the subject. Marberry joined us later and I caught him eyeing me curiously every now and then during the evening over our game of cribbage. I beat him three rubbers for a small consideration and went to my lodgings feeling better.

CHAPTER XVII.

THE FOOL

I don't know when it began, but along in March I found myself in a terribly gloomy condition. One day it came upon me like a revelation that I was unable, financially, to continue the kind of life I had been accustomed to. It was difficult to realize that my funds were reduced to a state that limited what I considered my reasonable wants. I had never kept such a thing as an account of personal expenditures, and I never really knew how big they were, weekly, monthly or annually. Though I had occasionally experienced the necessity of temporarily cutting them, down, overdue bills being my barometer. The cutting off of a large part of my income had been contemporaneous with the presentation of a number of bills which I could not meet, but it was some time before I realized that I could not look ahead and see any funds coming out of the future with which to meet them, and that, meanwhile, other obligations were growing up like rank weeds.

I had seen very little of Helen. I had never spoken of her to Kate. By unconscious steps I had come to believe that my career was ended, and that plans for my future welfare or happiness must all be declared off. I called occasionally at the Doctor's home, but spent most of my time at the clubs – and that was expensive. My real gloom and depression began when I thought I had discovered that not only was my career ended, but that it was getting every day further behindhand that debts were piling up, and besides that I was feeling, physically, very much out of form. After a time I had spells of pitying myself, and that was destructive. The thought of pitying myself made me feel vicious.

It was after one of these moods that I bought a revolver – a heavy, compact, shortmuzzled weapon. I don't think I realized what I bought it for, and I didn't want to think of it. Perhaps the sight of that pistol of Bowie's was responsible for the idea, I placed the weapon in a drawer of my dressing-case – another drawer from the one in which I kept the photograph of a sweet, sad face, that every night, now, I had come to look at.

The Fool

It was after a particularly gloomy talk with sympathetic Kate, one evening, that I returned to my rooms in an extraordinarily unenviable frame of mind – something as nearly akin to anguish as I had ever known. Kate had declared that I needed occupation. I had expressed to her how strange it seemed that the occupations for killing time, which I had enjoyed when I had something better to attend to and no time to kill, palled upon me now that I had nothing else to do. I had sold my horse and the modest rigs in my stable that day and discharged the man that took care of them. I sat down in my chamber by the open fireplace and wished that I was dead.

I don't know what time it was when I rose from the chair, walked over to the dressing-case and opened the drawer wherein lay the short-muzzled revolver. It had five chambers and a big cartridge faced me from each of the exposed chambers as I picked it up. I had had the weapon loaded when I bought it and had returned the broken box of leads to the dealer.

I turned the ugly thing in my hand and regarded it until it seemed to look less ugly, less fearful. Indeed, after a few moments it began to have a fascination for me, to be really attractive.

Then I put it down on top of the dressingcase and removed my jacket and vest. I placed my left hand over my heart and moved my little finger about until I could feel my heart beating directly beneath it. I went back to the dressing-case, picked up the revolver and felt for that heartbeat again with my left hand. The starched bosom of my shirt was in the way and I crushed it to one side. I found the spot, though it seemed as if the heart had wellnigh stopped beating. I worked the big mouth of the revolver under the tip of the finger over my heart and clinched the barrel in my hand to steady it.

I looked all about the room. My eyes rested for a moment on the front of the dressing-case drawer in which lay the photograph of that sweet, sad face. Helen's picture looked out at me from its frame on top of the dressing-case and I quickly turned my eyes from it. I saw in that glance around the room everything there was in it, the pictures, the books, the college diploma, the bits of bric-a-brac, my comfortable old slippers, a burnt match on the rug in front of the fireplace – everything. I let the revolver drop from my breast and then shut off the lights blazing from the gas brackets.

With the revolver clinched tightly in my right hand I made my way to the bed and lay down upon it. I felt for the heart -beat again with the fingers of my left hand.

CHAPTER XVIII.

AN INTERRUPTION

The quick thr-r-r-ink of an electric bell came to my ears. There was somebody at the door. I felt a sudden glow all over me. Then beads of perspiration broke out and face and body were wet. I raised myself half up from the bed, the revolver still in my hand. I heard the housekeeper go through the hall down-stairs. I heard a step on the stairs. I looked down at the revolver and shuddered. Ugh! what an ugly thing it was shining in the dark!

A knock on the door, a gentle tap – I threw the revolver across the room and it fell against something with an ugly bang and dropped with a muffled sound on a rug. I forgot that the room was dark, save for the glowing logs on the hearth, and I called "Come in!"

I saw a dim figure at the threshold – a woman's figure.

"Kate I" I cried. And I leaped from the bed and seizing her in my arms I dropped my head on her shoulder and burst into tears.

"Why, Dick!" exclaimed my sister. "Why, Dick! What is the matter? Were you asleep? Light the gas. You are trembling like a leaf – and crying. Dick! Dick!" her voice sounding full of fear. "What has happened. Light the gas and let me see you!"

I released her quickly and turned for a match. Then I thought of the revolver lying on the floor – somewhere, I didn't know where.

"No, no, Kate!" I cried. "Don't have the gas lighted. We can sit here by the fire, dear. I will start it up. I had a nightmare, I think – a nightmare! I threw myself on the bed – I was not asleep – only the nightmare," I repeated, my voice choking with the words. "Come, sit up by the fire. What on earth brings you here? I will start up the fire," and I proceeded to poke it and threw on a fresh log until it crackled into a blaze which brought my sister's face out clear – and mine, too.

"Why, Dick," she cried; "you are as white as a ghost!" I thought her voice betrayed an instinctive horror.

"Don't say a word to me, sister," I uttered, with a sort of a gasp. "Don't ask me anything. I'm sick. I'm not well – and the dream was awful. Sit down, dear. Why did you come here?" and of a sudden I felt almost irritated at her coming.

She told me, speaking rapidly, as if she wanted to be through with it to ask more of me. She said that she could not sleep without seeing me. She had a bundle with her which she told me contained a small fortune in negotiable securities, and she compelled me to take them from her.

"I have had them at the house for two days," she said. "You must take them. You must get into business – your old business if you can, but some business. You must not go on as you are. If there isn't enough there I have property that I can sell. You told me this would be enough to buy back the stock in your business. You must not refuse me."

"But, Kate," I put in, "you don't know what you are doing. This is your inheritance. It belongs to you. You must not surrender it both for your sake and your husband's; you must not sacrifice it."

"I may do as I please," declared my sister, stamping her foot. "I have talked it over with Edward, and he urged me to do it he did, really, Dick. We have enough, and we have no children, Dick," and my sister's voice faltered. "I have no one but you, Dick no one who is like a child to me but you, my little brother. I want you to begin over again. I know you cannot do it without money. And you must do it."

"And a pretty job I'm likely to make of it!" I declared, bitterly.

"I do not want you to lose it. I don't mean for my sake, but for your own. Yet I would hold you strictly responsible for it. I think you are the kind of a man who might take care of somebody else's money better than you do of your own. There is an element of honor in it, and I think you have honor."

Honor! I like to think I have it. I was never what the world calls dishonest.

"Kate," said I, after a pause. "I want you to do me a real favor. I want you to take these papers back home with you. I will come around to the house in a day or two and talk it over with yon. Meanwhile, I will consider it very seriously, and if, after all, you insist, I promise you to do what you tell me if I can possibly see my way clear to do it with any sort of justice."

"Don't talk about justice!" cried Kate. "I could not rest another night without seeing you, and making you let me help you. I ought to have insisted upon it before. But I have only lately come to know what a condition you were in. I can't let you make a wreck of yourself, and I'm afraid you cannot stand adversity as a strong man ought to."

I thought of the revolver lying on the floor some-where.

"Kate," said I, "you must go back home. I must get into bed. I am tired out awfully tired. I will put on my coat and go home with you."

She protested at this. She had come in Marberry's spyder, and the coachman was with her.

So I kissed her good-night and saw her down the front steps and into the jaunty spyder. Then I went back to my room, closed and locked the door.

I trembled as I crossed the room to strike a match and light the gas. I looked about me with a strange feel-ing of fear at what I should see. There lay the revolver on the heavy rug in front of the dressingcase.

I picked it up almost afraid to touch it. I threw clown the barrel and drew out the exposed cartridges, placing them in a corner of a drawer. Then I opened a window and hurled the weapon as far as I could throw it. I heard it come down with a clank upon the pavement 'way up the street.

I threw myself on the bed and buried my face in the pillow.

CHAPTER XIX.

NIGHT AND DAY

When I awoke it was broad daylight. The gas flame was burning. The logs on the hearth were reduced to smouldering embers. I was shivering from cold.

I raised myself up from the bed. My feet were numb and my shoes felt like cases of lead about them.

I looked down at my shirt at the starched bosom crushed and rumpled on the left side.

My head was aching terrifically. My very bones seemed to ache. When I attempted to step on the floor my legs were too weak to support me.

I sat down on the edge of the bed and rubbed my hands over my forehead and through my hair. My hair seemed dry and hot. There was an unpleasant taste in my mouth and my tongue felt thick and hot. My throat resisted the effort to swallow.

I worked off my shoes and began to disrobe. It was a painful operation. My fingers were weak and sore. I found my pajamas lying over the footboard where the housemaid had placed them the evening before. I got into them and touched the electric button located in the wall conveniently close. When the maid responded I asked her to make me a cocktail. She makes a very fair cocktail for an emergency, having had a number of emergency experiences since she has been with me.

But somehow the cocktail did not taste as good as I expected it would, and I asked her to fetch me some tea and toast

I lay in bed and slept a little during the day. Toward night I had the maid telephone for Doctor Tom, and when the Doctor came he told me I must lie where I was until he gave me permission to get up.

I don't know how long I lay there. It seemed months. Kate came over immediately on hearing that I was sick and insisted on employing a nurse. I begged her not to do it, but that night I asked the Doctor to get word to Helen – not to send for her, nor tell her directly, but arrange some device to have her learn that I was sick. I don't know how he went about it, but one evening Helen came in. She came alone and she said very little. She stayed until eleven o'clock, sat by my bedside and helped me to the Doctor's medicine. I think she came every evening for the many weeks. I can't recall much from those weeks except that I thought I knew when she was by my bedside. I slept much of the time, perhaps. The housemaid proved to be a very good nurse, and Kate was with me during the afternoons – nearly every afternoon, I think. So we got along very nicely.

One evening I opened my eyes with a feeling as if I had just waked from a long nap – a sleep full of horrible dreams that I could not picture to myself, but was confident that they had been horrible. I turned my head on the pillow, and then a figure advanced swiftly and noiselessly from across the room. It was Helen. She bent over me and looked into mv eyes.

"Why don't you speak, Helen?" I said, looking at her with a strange feeling of curiosity as to what her presence meant, and why she was sober and silent.

Helen started as if my voice startled her. Indeed, I thought she was a bit frightened.

"Why don't you speak, Helen?" I repeated.

"Why, Dick!" she cried out, and then dropping her voice almost to a whisper, "You are better, aren't you, Dick? The Doctor said last evening you were going to be better – or – or – "

"Or die, Helen? I suppose I have been mighty sick, haven't I, Helen?" It seemed strange, the sound of my own voice.

"Very sick, Dick. And you are very weak, now. I don't think you ought to talk about it."

"But, Helen," I persisted, with a sort of gladness that I was talking, "have you been with me all the time, Helen?"

''Every evening, Dick.''

And all the night, for a good many nights, as I afterward learned.

"And who else has been here?"

"Not many people. The Doctor wouldn't let any one see you but Jennie, the maid, and your sister."

"My sister – Kate? And – and – have you seen Kate?"

"Of course – what a sweet woman she is. She was very good to me."

"Good to you, Helen! She couldn't be otherwise, you dear little woman. And the boys – have any of the fellows asked after me?"

"Lots of them, Dick and have sent you Things – things to eat and funny bottles of wine and things to drink," and Helen laughed a soft little laugh.

"And I couldn't eat the things they sent to eat nor drink the stuff in the funny bottles, I suppose, Helen?" and I laughed, too, weakly enough.

"Of course not. But it was very nice of them, though, I'm sure. And Mrs. Marberry has brought you flowers – the flowers are beginning to grow out of doors, now, you know, Dick."

I looked over at the hearth. No fire was blazing there, but the room was warm and I noticed a window open.

I turned over on my side – it was a mighty effort, and Helen sat down in a chair that stood at the head of the bed. I drew one arm from under the bedclothes and reached out my hand toward her. The hand was awfully thin and white.

Helen met it with a warm little grasp that seemed to make the blood rush into the chilly fingers.

"Helen," I said, feeling very weak and my voice almost failing me, "if I ever get well and strong, I shall want to tell you that I love you. Will you let me, then?"

"Of course, Dick." Her voice was very low and gentle.

"Mayn't I tell you it now, Helen?"

"If you wish to, Dick," and her eyes filled with tears as she looked into mine.

"I do want to, Helen," I said, "because I love you. You have been awfully good to me, little woman. I love you."

Helen bent over and kissed me.

"And I love you, Dick," she said.

CHAPTER XX.

THE LAST CONFESSION

I am sitting in a great big roomy chamber in the Doctor's house, up-country. Despite my horror of the country, I have had a remarkably pleasant visit and shall go back to town, to-morrow, with a new health and strength – a new kind, I hope.

Through the open window I see the great hills, a long range, green clad, over the edge of which the new moon is just disappearing. The sky is full of twinkling stars.

The old maples about the house are soughing in the gentle breeze. There is the musical sound of rushing water and the unbroken rustle of a little waterfall from the back of the house; and in its pools the trout are sleeping.

There is no other sound, none but the soughing boughs and the rushing stream and the water falling,

falling. It is appallingly still. The chamber is filled with the fragrance of honeysuckles about the porch.

I rise from the window and light a candle that stands on the old-fashioned bureau. Helen's picture is there, in its frame. And in the top drawer is another picture – the portrait of a sweet, sad face. I take it out and, holding it by the candle's light, look at it.

I know you would be fond of Helen, sweet, sad girl. Sometimes I think Helen is like you – only Helen is not sad – and she shall never be!

You are dead, sweet girl.

The Doctor told me that you wore your life out.

I know what he meant.

He meant that I wore your life out.

I know that you died of neglect, poor love my girl-wife.

THE END.

www.ingramcontent.com/pod-product-compliance
Lightning Source LLC
Chambersburg PA
CBHW071607040426
42452CB00008B/1268